Bert Bielefeld

Building
Contract

Bert Bielefeld

Building
Contract

BIRKHÄUSER
BASEL

Contents

FOREWORD _7

INTRODUCTION _9

TYPES OF CONTRACTS _11
Awarding contracts to individual trades _11
Awarding contracts to general contractors _14
Measurement contract _18
Lump sum contract _20
Alternative types of contracts _22

CONTRACTUAL PROVISIONS _23
Rights and duties of parties to the contract _24
Deadlines _25
Remuneration _29
Payment _30
Variation orders _31
Acceptance _34
Liability and insurance _35
Security _36
Dispute resolution mechanisms _38

CONTRACT COMPONENTS _40
Description of work / services _42
Design documents, expert reports _45
Other components _49

CONTRACTING PROCEDURES _51
Objectives and principles _51
Procedure leading to awarding a contract _53
Measures associated with the building work _56
Documentation _60

CONCLUSION _62

APPENDIX _63
Model contracts _63
Literature _64

Foreword

Usually, as a student or starting out in the profession, one has little project or site experience. Perhaps one has gained an initial insight into the work of a design practice or the operations of a construction site during an internship; however, dealing with construction contracts is not usually at the top of the agenda. *Basics Building Contract* is aimed at students and those starting out in the profession at this stage of their knowledge and, with the help of easily understood introductions and explanations, analyzes the key elements and content of construction contracts in a structured manner. The book clearly illustrates the constituents of a good building contract: the choice of a suitable type of contract, assessing contractual risks, a clearly structured and project-specific contract design, and, finally, well-functioning amendment and conflict management. Understanding the types of building contracts, their provisions and components, is an essential tool of the architect, from the first decisions regarding a project through to the professional handover to the client. It goes without saying that this book cannot replace actual professional experience, but it can be used to gain a deep practical and structured comprehension that will enable the reader to understand the contractual context between client and building contractor independent of existing contract templates, such as those in Section B of the German Construction Contract Procedures (VOB), or FIDIC.

Bert Bielefeld, Editor

Introduction

Various different design and building processes have to take place before a building is fully designed and completed. As a first step, the framework conditions of the project have to be defined; then an optimal design has to be developed to suit these framework conditions. This concept must then be further developed, taking into account all specialist engineering designs for structure, services installations, and so forth, to the point where building permits can be obtained for the project. Drawings and documents have to be produced as the basis of the building execution and for the specifications in order to determine various aspects of the level of quality. These are used to obtain quotations from building contractors so that the building work can be awarded to and placed with the best bidder.

This then results in a building contract to be concluded between the client and the building contractor. This building contract can take various quite different forms: it can be the result of a short commissioning letter from the client, take the form of a template for a building contract stipulated by the client, or can be agreed to in extensive negotiations between the contract parties.

In larger projects, the client usually involves lawyers, who will formulate the building contract and may also carry out the negotiations. Independent of the above, it is necessary and essential that architects advise their clients prior to and during the tendering procedure for building work and provide support during this process. Decisions have to be made about the different ways of drafting the contract; it is also important to make the right decisions for the project at the outset, and to align the design, the specifications, and finally the tender procedure with those decisions. Important decisions include where the building work is to be placed, whether the building work is to be placed with the different trades or with just one general contractor, and how the client wishes the building project to be described in the building contract, i.e. in a general functional form or with technical details. This results in different approaches when still at the design stage, which means that budding and practicing architects need to know the different types of building contracts and the way they can be modified.

As a rule, it is not possible to reproduce construction contracts using templates because projects vary so much in terms of function, type, and size, the tendering procedure, the commercial conditions, and many other aspects. Ultimately, the parameters determining a project in detail always have to be re-established and fixed (set) in a building contract. An important distinction exists between construction contracts for private, commercial, and public clients, because public clients in particular are subject to strict rules regarding the tender procedure and awarding of building contracts.

A good building contract that is appropriate for the specific project is an important prerequisite for a smooth and effective construction process with as few disruptions and escalations as possible, and is hence a key element for a successful project. For this reason, the following chapters cover all the important types, properties, and contents of construction contracts that are needed by architects for carrying out design and building projects. We will not be discussing the details of standard building contracts, but will explain generally applicable types of contracts and provisions, as well as their background and objectives. This is intended to generate a deeper understanding of mutual dependencies between client and building contractor, independent of the application of standard contracts such as those provided in the VOB/B, FIDIC, and NEC.

Types of contracts

Building contracts can be divided into different categories according to their different emphases and purposes. As a first step, it is necessary to differentiate between building contracts and architects' and engineers' agreements, which deal mainly with the design and supervision of the project. From a simplified legal point of view, clients need architects and engineers to formulate and define their design and quality requirements for building contractors. Since the results of the architectural and engineering design become the basis of the building contract, the architects and engineers are acting as the client's agents from the point of view of the building contractor. > Fig. 1 In cases where the client does not commission the complete design of the building work before placing the contract, there will be architects and engineers working on the contractor's side whose task it is to complete the design ready for building.

Distinction between architects' agreements and building contracts

In building contracts, the scope of work and method of accounting can vary widely. For example, building work may be placed with individual tradespeople or all the building work may be placed with a single general contractor. Furthermore, it is possible to pay for the construction work on the basis of labor and materials actually used for the project, or on a lump sum basis.

AWARDING CONTRACTS TO INDIVIDUAL TRADES

Traditionally, contracts for building work are awarded individually to tradespeople such as carpenters, floor-layers, or painters and decorators. This results from the fact that tradespeople learn their professions over many years, and offer the work associated with their specific trade in the market. This means that the work is available in the structure of

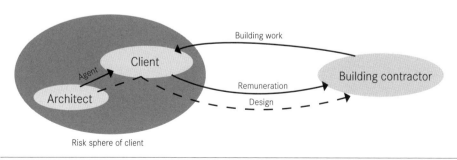

Fig. 1: The principle of architect as agent in building contracts and architects' agreements

the different trade sections and can therefore be called up and commissioned accordingly by the client. > Fig. 2

Individual trade
tender/trade

This method of awarding contracts is sometimes referred to as individual trade tendering. The term "individual trade tender" or "trade" refers to work that falls into the remit of a particular trade. In Germany, the most common award procedure is the individual trade tender procedure; in many other countries, it is more common to place contracts with general contractors. The following list covers the main kinds of work that fall under the remit of specific trades:

— Foundations
— Drilling work
— Shoring work
— Bricklaying/masonry/artificial stonework
— Concrete and reinforced concrete work
— Steel construction work
— Landscaping
— Carpentry (timber houses, roofs, framing, etc.)
— Sealing work (sealing against ground moisture, groundwater, etc.)
— Roofing and flashing work/gutters and eavestroughs/soffits
— Window work (windows, fittings, glazing, etc.)
— Scaffolding
— Plaster and stucco work
— Drywall construction work
— Floor and wall tiling
— Screed work
— Parquet flooring work
— Floor finishing work (carpets, linoleum, laminate, etc.)
— Joinery (furniture, wooden doors, etc.)
— Metalwork (staircases, metal doors, etc.)
— Painting and decorating work
— Heating, gas, and ventilation and air-conditioning work (HVAC)
— Plumbing/sanitary installation work
— Electrical installation work
— Lightning protection work
— Elevator and conveyor technology

Number of
contract partners

In the case of individual trade tendering, between 20 and 30 different contractors may be involved in order to complete the building. As a result, this method involves numerous awarding processes, as well as numerous building contracts. Within the same project, these building contracts will be similar in structure; nevertheless, specific contract conditions and contract provisions have to be established and agreed upon for each individual trade.

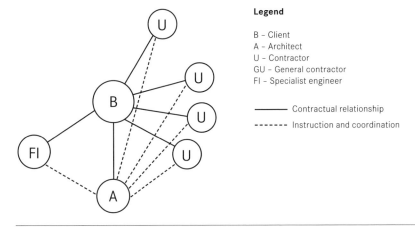

Fig. 2: Principle of individual trade tendering

This means that the client and architect must be highly competent in knowing the specialized fields and in their ability to coordinate, because the client (often through the architect) is responsible for the supervision and coordination of the work of all the trades involved. This also means that the client and architect carry the risk of coordination and can only allocate the responsibility for any delays in the construction process to the building contractors if delays are the direct result of internal processes within the trade. Furthermore, it follows that individual trade tendering will take up a considerable amount of time.

However, on the positive side, there is the fact that the client can choose each individual trade enterprise, which is not possible when a general contractor is appointed. In other words, the client can decide which trade enterprise will perform the work cost efficiently, on time, to a high standard of quality, and with a willingness to oblige. Another advantage lies in the fact that the client, with the help of the architect, can have better control of the finished quality of the work and can even ask for adjustments to be made. Overall, the client therefore has much greater freedom in the designing and decision-making than with the general contractor award procedure.

In order to limit the number of contracted companies, it is possible to award in packages. In this procedure, several trades are combined into an award unit.

Advantages and disadvantages

Awarding of packages

○

○ **Note:** The term "award unit" refers to all work and services allocated to a contract partner in a building contract. This can therefore include the work of individual or several trades or the entire building work.

This has the advantage that the client has to carry out fewer awarding procedures; it also often makes sense to integrate the trades that
● have critical coordination interfaces into one single award unit.

A prerequisite for awarding packages is that there must be enough suppliers of the respective package in the market who can offer this work. For this reason, one should not form unusual packages involving completely unrelated types of work.

AWARDING CONTRACTS TO GENERAL CONTRACTORS

The most common alternative to awarding to individual trades is awarding to general contractors. In this case, the necessary building work for fully completing a building is placed with a single building contractor. Here, the general contractor (GC) is the sole contract partner for all building work.

Subcontractors

This general contractor will then have to subcontract all work and services the company cannot carry out by itself to other building companies or trades. These secondary contractors are referred to as subcon-
○ tractors.

Timing of awards

Individual trade contracts are normally not awarded until the architect has completed the design to the point where the trades can implement the construction drawings directly. By contrast, the award to a general contractor can take place at various points in time. If the architect has completed the design to the same extent needed for individual trade tendering, the award of the contract to a general contractor usually only covers the actual building work and service – in other words, all the building work is combined into one package.

Inclusion of design services

If, however, a general contractor is appointed *during the design process*, it is usual for this contractor to also provide design services in order to complete the design to a stage where it can be implemented. For example, the award can take place at the following stages of the process:
> Fig. 3

— Completed detailed design → GC only contracted for building work / services > Fig. 4
— Project approved with main details → GC contracted for building work + specialist engineers > Fig. 5

● **Example:** Bricklaying and reinforced concrete work are usually combined in the shell construction package. If appropriate, it is possible to expand this package by adding foundations, scaffolding work, and sealing work.

○ **Note:** It is very common nowadays for general contractors themselves not to carry out any operative building work, i.e. they no longer employ their own operatives but place all work and services with subcontractors. Whereas German uses a different term for this type of contractor (Generalübernehmer), in English the term "general contractor" applies either way.

- Schematic design completed → GC contracted for building work + detailed design + specialist engineers
- No design → GC contracted to produce design + building work/ services + specialist engineers > Fig. 6   O

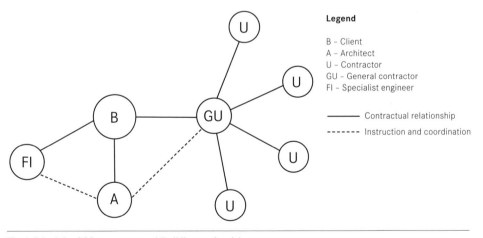

Detailed design completed | Start of construction

Outline design | Building approval

Start of design

Design and building process

Client: room schedule
GC: design + build

Client: outline design
GC: continuation of design + build

Client: approval, schematic design
GC: architect, specialist engineers + build

Client: approval, schematic design
GC: specialist engineers + build

Client: complete design
GC: build only

Fig. 3: Timing of contract award to a general contractor in relation to the stage of design completion

Legend

B – Client
A – Architect
U – Contractor
GU – General contractor
FI – Specialist engineer

——— Contractual relationship
- - - - - Instruction and coordination

Fig. 4: Principle of GC contract award (building work only)

O **Note:** In cases where the client does not commission his own architect to carry out design services but commissions a general contractor to handle the complete package, the contractor is referred to as "design-and-build contractor."

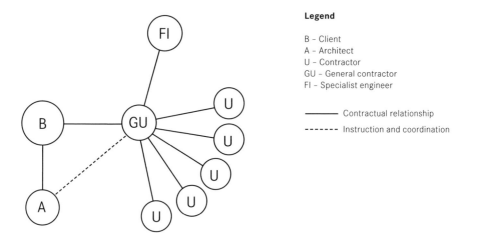

Legend

B – Client
A – Architect
U – Contractor
GU – General contractor
FI – Specialist engineer

——— Contractual relationship
------- Instruction and coordination

Fig. 5: Principle of GC contract award with main details (including specialist engineer's design)

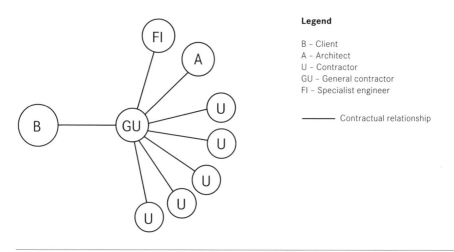

Legend

B – Client
A – Architect
U – Contractor
GU – General contractor
FI – Specialist engineer

——— Contractual relationship

Fig. 6: Principle of GC contract award with no design (including building design and specialist engineer's design)

Award of additional services · Beyond the above, it is not uncommon these days to place contracts that include significantly more services than those of the original design and construction phases. This may include the funding of projects, in which case general contractors form consortiums with banks and thereby undertake another organizational task on behalf of the client. Another option is for operating and commissioning tasks to be included, so that the general contractor takes on the operation of the building on a permanent basis or for a defined transitional period, during which the technical systems are fine-tuned, and then hands over the tried-and-tested project to the client. Such contractual constellations are often chosen for infrastructure and civil engineering projects, as well as plant installations (e.g. sewage works, power stations), with the idea of benefiting from the general contractor's specialist knowledge of operations.

If it is intended that the general contractor will participate permanently, or at least for a longer period of time, in the project, it is common to form joint company structures in which client and general contractor cooperate. A typical example used by public clients is the Public Private Partnership (PPP). A number of different models are available, which differ in their ownership provisions, income distribution, and utilization risk:

PPP projects

- PPP owner model: the public client remains the owner of the building and the GC completes the construction and enters into a use contract with the public client
- PPP purchaser model: the GC builds and operates the building on his own land and enters into a lease-purchase contract with the public client
- PPP tenancy model: the GC designs and builds on his own land; he leases the property to the public client but retains ownership and the property reverts to him at the end of the tenancy
- PPP lease-to-own model: as above, but at the end of the tenancy the client becomes the owner of the property
- PPP concession model: the GC has the right to charge fees for the operation and the building (e.g. in the case of private motorway/highway operators)
- PPP contracting model: the GC takes on the installation and optimization of a technical plant in the owner's building and can draw capital against this as part of a fixed consideration negotiated beforehand
- PPP company model: the GC and client together form a project-specific company and arrange the joint project, including its maintenance, via company agreements

Another option for the awarding of comprehensive services to a contractor is via a developer contract. In this situation, the client purchases a completed building (usually including the land), which has yet to be built. This provides the client with the advantage of not having to deal with the design and construction phases, and being able to purchase a "complete" building at a fixed price. In contrast to the purchase of an existing property, the client is able to influence the design and quality of the finishes of the building.

Developer contract

MEASUREMENT CONTRACT

Irrespective of the scope of the work and services assigned to a building contractor, building contracts can be distinguished by the type of accounting and remuneration. In a measurement contract, or a unit price contract, the quantities of the work likely to be furnished or provided are estimated at the tendering stage. These quantities are conveyed to the contractor in the specifications during the tender procedure so that the contractor's cost calculator can estimate the volume of the work to be provided. > Fig. 7 These quantities do not form the basis of the remuneration; instead, the quantities actually produced as part of the construction process are then measured and form the basis of the final account.

○ This means that the contract is only based on the agreed *unit prices*.

The quantity risk lies with the client

Since payment is made for the quantity actually supplied, the quantity risk lies with the client. Should the estimated quantity change, the client will have to pay any additional costs that may arise; if, on the other hand, the quantities are less than estimated, the client benefits from reduced costs. The building contractor is fully remunerated for all contractual quantities required for the building and furnished by him, even if the

● quantities estimated at the time of the tender process were not correct.

Review of accounts

When the building contractor wants to be paid for his output during or after completion of the work, he will have to provide evidence in his invoices of the actual furnished quantities, based on measurements, drawings, etc. These measurements are then examined by the supervising architect and form the basis of the final contract sum, which the client then pays to the contractor.

○ **Note:** The term "unit price" refers to the price payable for a piece, a square meter, a linear meter, etc., as offered by the building contractor. The quantity actually supplied is then multiplied by the unit price, resulting in the final amount to be paid.

● **Example:** Deviations from the estimated quantities can be caused by computation errors during the design or by unforeseen events on the building site. For example, if an estimate was made during the design stage as to how much excavation was required for loose soil and how much for rock, it is quite possible for the actual quantities to deviate significantly.

2. Interior fit-out
   2.1 Drywalling work
      2.1.4 Sheetrock walls, 125 mm   Quantity   Unit price   Total price
      Sheetrock wall, metal studs, alu-C profiles,
      lined on both sides (each 2 × 12.5 mm sheetrock board),
      60 mm gap filled with mineral wool, skimmed and
      sanded (Q3)
      Height: 2.85 m
      Product designation: XXX (or equivalent)
      If different product, state make:

                                    82 m²

Example of bill of quantities

---

2. Interior fit-out
   2.1 Drywalling work
      2.1.4 Sheetrock walls, 125 mm   Quantity   Unit price   Total price
      Sheetrock wall, metal studs, alu-C profiles,
      lined on both sides (each 2 × 12.5 mm sheetrock board),
      60 mm gap filled with mineral wool, skimmed and
      sanded (Q3)
      Height: 2.85 m
      Product designation: XXX (or equivalent)
      If different product, state make:

                                    82 m²   45.00 €   3690.00 €

Example of bill of quantities with prices

---

1. Shell construction

2. Interior fit-out
   2.1. Drywalling work
      2.1.4 Sheetrock walls, 125 mm   Actual   Unit price   Total price
                                           quantity

                                         86 m²   45.00 €   3870.00 €

   3. Installation

Example of invoice based on bill of quantities (detailed text omitted)

Fig. 7: Examples of an item in a unit price contract in the tender and final account stages

LUMP SUM CONTRACT

In contrast to the above, in a lump sum contract the building contractor bears the quantity risk, irrespective of whether the work was specified in detail or described in more general functional terms. > Chapter Contract components, Description of work/services The client pays a lump sum and thereby reduces his risk, but cannot benefit from reduced costs where the actual quantities delivered are less than the number estimated.

Consolidation of quantities
It is important, however, to understand that only the quantities of units, and hence their remuneration, are consolidated. The overall work output is not consolidated, which means that any deviation from the agreed-upon work must be paid for, irrespective of the type of contract. Work output can only be transferred in a global way if it is functionally described as the result of work input.

Lump sum contracts are distinguished by the two methods of describing the work/services:

— Detailed lump sum contracts
— Global lump sum contracts

Detailed lump sum contracts
Detailed lump sum contracts are not significantly different from measurement contracts. In both types of contracts, the work is described in detail (usually in the form of specifications). However, the quantities are not taken into account in detailed lump sum contracts. If they are measured, they serve merely as information in the awarding process. In a detailed lump sum contract, the total lump sum is contractually agreed upon, rather than the unit prices. > Fig. 8

Global lump sum contracts
As a rule, global lump sum contracts are based on a functional description of the work to be provided. This means that the description consists essentially of the objectives and quality requirements of the client, without any exact details as to how this is to be implemented in terms of building construction. > Chapter Contract components, Description of work/services The later in the design process that the contract is awarded, > Fig. 3 the greater will be the detail and the scope of descriptions in the design documents and specifications. Because the description is only global, the building contractor has to shoulder not only the quantity risk, but also more risk in terms of the overall building output. In this situation, it is usually difficult to allocate individual payments to actual work furnished, because the contractor has offered such work with only one or a few lump sum prices. This makes it difficult to check variation orders where there have been changes to the required work output, and also to accurately estimate the completion stage for the purpose of stage payments.

Accounting procedure in lump sum contracts
As a general principle, payment for work is only made by the client for work done, in order to ensure that the building contractor is not overpaid. With lump sum contracts, it is therefore important for the supervising architect to assess the actual amount of work done at the various

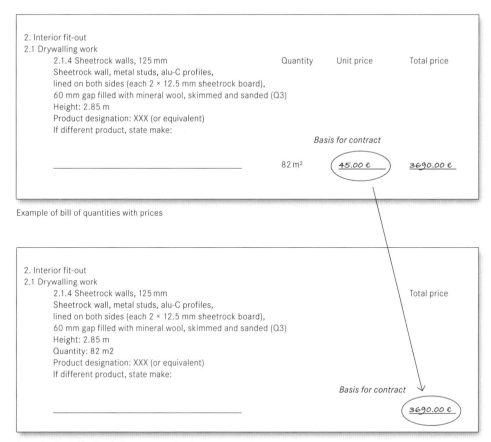

Example of bill of quantities with prices

Example of specification for lump sum contract

Fig. 8: Consolidation of a specification item

stages. Whereas with detailed lump sum contracts it is relatively easy to check an invoice owing to the split prices, this is harder in the case of global lump sum contracts, since it is difficult to allocate the general lump sum prices to the work output. One way to achieve this is with the help of an original cost calculation and the partial lump sums disclosed in the tender; alternatively, the building contractor submits a guarantee to the client which, in the case of overpayment, reimburses the client with the difference so that staged payments can be made irrespective of the actual stage of completion.

In order to simplify the accounting procedure of global lump sum contracts, it is common to agree upon payment plans that establish consolidated remuneration packages based on the construction schedule and the submitted cost calculation. These packages are then contractually agreed to in a payment plan.

Payment plans

ALTERNATIVE TYPES OF CONTRACTS

In addition to measurement and lump sum contracts, there are various other types of contracts; however, these are not very common in practice and are based at least in part on the same basic principles of these two types of contracts. By way of example, three versions are described below.

Hourly rate contract In the hourly rate contract, the hours worked are remunerated. This is particularly suitable for small projects or for work that cannot be comprehensively described and calculated, and consists primarily of labor, as in the repair of an existing property. Any cost of materials and equipment is remunerated separately.

Open book The term "open book" refers to an agreement in which the contractor's cost calculation is laid open to both contract partners. The building contractor shows the respective cost of each individual item in the cost calculation, and also discloses his additions for site overheads, general business overheads, and profit. (This type of contract is sometimes called "cost-plus," a reference to the pricing process.) On this basis, it is easy to draw up and examine changes to the contract/variation orders. This procedure is particularly useful in projects in which the work output cannot be comprehensively described.

Guaranteed maximum price The guaranteed maximum price (GMP) is a lump sum contract which includes an incentive system. The building contractor guarantees a lump sum price (the maximum price), but is encouraged to reduce costs. The difference is then split between the client and building contractor in contractually agreed-upon proportions, creating a win-win situation.

Contractual provisions

In very basic terms, a building contract consists of two components, one of them to be supplied by the client and the other by the contractor. The client contributes the description of all necessary work and services, and the framework conditions for dealing with the construction and contract. This can be referred to as the deliverables. The contractor contributes his tender bid, in which he supplies tendered prices for the work/services required by the client. This can be referred to as the payables. These two components – deliverables and payables – are the elementary parts of every building contract. > Fig. 9

In addition, certain arrangements for handling or managing the building contract must be laid out within the contractual relationship between client and contractor. These "rules of play" or standard practices include the general rights and duties of the contract parties and also the framework conditions and processes of execution. This section deals with the most important provisions to be agreed upon in a building contract.

Deliverables/
payables

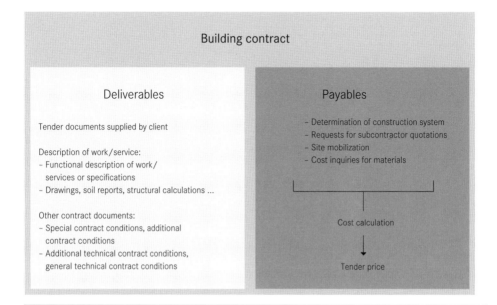

Fig. 9: Deliverables/payables

RIGHTS AND DUTIES OF PARTIES TO THE CONTRACT

Each party to the contract has rights and duties; these must be properly discharged to ensure the success of the building project. The most elementary duty of the building contractor is to provide the building work, and that of the client is to accept the work output and pay for it. > Tab. 1

Duty to cooperate and provide information

Beyond the most elementary duties of the two parties, there are secondary duties, such as the duty to cooperate, the duty to provide information, and the duty to limit damage, which are instrumental in ensuring smooth interactions between the two parties to the contract. The duty to cooperate on the part of the client includes, for example, providing the design documents and the construction site to the building contractor.

Likewise, the building contractor has a duty to cooperate, for example, in providing information to the client about the work or about the products used in the building process. Furthermore, if problems arise, the contractor has a duty to help limit any damage in order to keep delays as short as possible.

Right of instruction

Usually the building contract assigns the right of instruction to the client, enabling him to make necessary adjustments to the specified work. Since it is not always possible to foresee all events that can occur during the building process, the right of instruction is necessary for bringing the project to a successful conclusion.

As a general principle, it is important for the building contractor to have the duty to carry out this necessary work under the client's right of instruction. However, as a rule there are contractual limitations to this.

Tab. 1: Essential rights and duties of parties to the contract

	Rights	Duties
Client (ordering party)	— Right of instruction — General right to terminate	— Duty of remuneration — Duty of acceptance — Provision of design and building site (duty to cooperate) — Damage limitation duty
Contractor (executing party)	— Right to terminate for good reason	— Duty to supply work / services (the agreed-upon building work) — Duty to supply information — Duty to provide evidence of the quality of the work / services — Damage limitation duty

● **Example:** When a client commissions a decorator, the decorator must be given access to the surfaces to be decorated, notwithstanding the client's option to rely on other trades such as those for shell construction, plastering, or drywalling for the purpose of providing this access.

● **Example:** The groundwork for excavating the building pit or cavity is awarded on the basis of the expert soil analysis report. During the excavation work it is possible that unexpected events may occur, such as obstacles in the ground, contamination, different types of soil, or unexpected artesian water. In order to ensure that the construction work can proceed, the client must be able to give the necessary instructions, which in this case could not be covered by the agreed-upon work output.

Should the client make excessive use of his right of instruction to an extent that is no longer related to the fulfillment of the contractually agreed-upon performance (defect-free building as per the building contract), the building contractor must be granted the right to refuse to do such work/service.

If one party to the contract refuses to carry out their contractual duty or does not fulfill such duty even after having been reminded, the other party normally has the right to give notice of termination. If, following receipt of the invoice and a reminder, the client does not make payment on the justified demand, the building contractor can stop work and, if appropriate, terminate the contract. Conversely, the client can terminate the contract if the building contractor does not carry out the work in a timely manner, or the work rendered is riddled with defects. Often the client also has a one-sided right of termination without default on the part of the building contractor; the purpose of this is to give the client an opportunity, for example, to get out of a project that he cannot see through to the end. However, in most cases, this does not free the client from the obligation to make partial payment for the work that was not done because of the cancellation. As a rule, the exact rights and effects of termination are specified in the contract.

○ Right of termination

DEADLINES

Other important components of every building contract are deadlines and time limits. Deadlines normally refer to specific dates, whereas time limits refer to periods of time, usually periods of time within which certain work has to be completed. It is possible to include deadlines or time limits for the building contractor's execution and also time limits for the handing over of drawings, for passing approval, or for making payments. A general distinction should be made as to whether deadlines and time limits have been set only for information purposes (for example, in the form of a time schedule attached to the tender documents) or whether they form a firm part of the contract (so-called contractual deadlines). Non-binding execution deadlines are intended to make it possible for the building contractor, during the tender phase, to estimate the effort and time involved in planning and coordination. For this reason, it is common to include an updated time schedule; the actual execution deadlines are then agreed to as contractual deadlines during the contract negotiations.

○ **Note:** As a rule, the rights of instruction, performance, and refusal are defined by legal provisions or the respective model contracts, such as those in the VOB/B, FIDIC, or NEC. Should these rights not be defined by reference to an established regulatory instrument, the limits between the duty to perform following justified instruction and the right to refuse following unjustified instruction must be clearly defined.

Contractual deadlines are always binding on the respective parties. For example, fixed deadlines for handing over drawings or for providing access to the building site would be obligatory for the client, while the building contractor must complete the work by a specific date. Contractual deadlines can be agreed upon as start dates, intermediate dates, and final completion dates. For the purpose of intermediate deadlines, it is advisable to define the required work quite precisely so that it will be possible to assess whether the deadline has been met. > Fig. 10

In some cases, contractually binding deadlines are linked to contractual penalties should the deadlines not be met. This is intended to increase the pressure on the contractor, who has to expect financial disadvantages in the case of a delay. However, contractual penalties may not be used to unreasonably reduce the justified and appropriate remuneration of the contractor. For this reason, they are usually limited to a maximum of 5% of the overall volume.

Once the contracts have been concluded, building contractors must always be given a certain period of time to carry out work preparation. Normally, building contractors have to order materials, which then have to be delivered to the construction site; they have to plan the deployment of their employees and machinery and, if appropriate, mobilize the building site and erect cranes. The minimum period to be allowed for this should not be less than two weeks between conclusion of the building contract and the start of construction, provided always that the building contractor has the necessary capacity available. When materials are ordered or prefabricated away from the construction site, the time period required may be significantly longer.

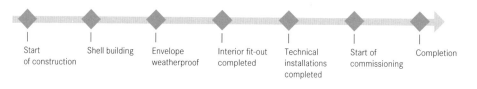

| Start of construction | Shell building | Envelope weatherproof | Interior fit-out completed | Technical installations completed | Start of commissioning | Completion |

Fig. 10: Typical contractual dates/deadlines

● **Example:** If the intermediate deadline is defined as "Heating system completed," it is not clear whether the heating system just has to be installed, or must be fully functional, or even in operation. Likewise, the milestone sometimes called "Building weathertight," which is so important for the interior fit-out or finishing, does not specify whether all windows and doors have to be installed/fitted or whether the building can be made weathertight with boarded walls/window openings and temporary doors.

○ **Note:** Contractual penalties are also sometimes referred to as "just penalties." Penalties must only be imposed when the delay is clearly within the sphere of risk of the contractor. In the case of individual contracts with many tradespeople it is often difficult to provide evidence of this, owing to the mutual dependencies. For this reason, contractual penalties cannot always be implemented in practice.

As a rule, the due dates or time periods for execution are also agreed upon as part of the building contract. In addition to the overall period allowed for execution, intermediate due dates are often agreed upon. This is particularly desirable when critical time-related interfaces with other trades exist. However, one should not agree to too many intermediate due dates, since this could make flexible coordination of the work more difficult.

Due dates and time periods for execution

When execution due dates are agreed upon, it is important to take into account the duty to cooperate on various matters, for example:

■
Cooperation in agreeing due dates

— The date for providing access to the construction site
— The handover date for drawings and other documents by the client/architect
— The handover date for drawings and other documents by the building contractor to the client for examination and approval
— The date for handover of documents and information on building materials and other structures
— The processes for viewing and examining submitted documents
— The processes for inspecting materials and surfaces
— The provision of staff or materials
— The coordination, and assisting with the coordination, of the work

Detailed provisions regarding the above items are made in particular for larger building projects in order to establish regular procedures and to prevent hold-ups.

Interferences or disruptions are not uncommon in the building process so it makes sense to include mechanisms for dealing with these in the building contract. As a general principle, the building contractor has a duty of cooperation to limit damage in order to minimize the effects of disruptions as much as possible.

Obstruction notice

Examples of interference/disruption in the construction process:

— Unexpected climate conditions such as sudden cold, frost, or non-stop rain
— *Force majeure* such as flooding or earthquake

> ■ **Tip:** As a rule, it makes more sense to agree upon execution periods rather than due dates, and to set the date for the anticipated start of the work. This is because, in the case of complications/interference/ disruptions or modifications, the agreed-upon periods are likely to remain valid, unlike fixed due dates which, in the case of delays, can only be used indirectly to calculate new due dates.

- Lack of cooperation on the part of the client
- Delays by previous trades
- Construction site obstructed by materials of other trades, waste, etc.
- Conditions on site deviating from the design, such as in the case of geological deviations from the design
- Damage to already-completed components, theft, etc.

Obstruction notice   It is essential that the building contractor inform the client immediately in the case of interference with or obstruction of the building work, to give the client a chance to respond. The so-called obstruction notice includes information on the interference/disruption, as well as a detailed description of the item that is obstructing the work and of how long the interference is likely to last. The purpose of an obstruction notice is to give the client enough information to enable him to understand the framework conditions and to eliminate the interference as quickly as possible. > Fig. 11

Client

Hans Meier
11 Anyroad
Anytown 54123

Any Construction Company Ltd.

Contact
Erika Anyone

Telephone:
01234 - 56789
Fax:
01234 - 567890

30.01.2018

Obstruction notice in accordance with Section 6 No. 1 VOB/B

Dear Madam, Sir

We herewith notify you in accordance with Section 6, para. 1 VOB/B, of the fact that we are currently obstructed in the proper execution of the work assigned to us. May we point out that the obstructing circumstances are within your field of risk. The causes are as follows:

- Work to be furnished by other companies for the health and safety of our employees has not been completed (scaffolding, provision of site electricity)

In accordance with Section 6, para. 2 VOB/B, the agreed time period for execution should therefore be appropriately extended. In view of the fact that the duration of the obstruction cannot be conclusively assessed at this stage, we cannot clearly determine the extent of the extension required for the execution period. We will come back to this as soon as the cause of the obstruction has been removed.

With kind regards,

Any Construction Company Ltd.

Fig. 11: Example of an obstruction notice

It may also be useful, beyond the obstruction notice itself, to determine standard procedures of how to proceed in the case of disruptions in order to prevent disputes at a later date.

REMUNERATION

An important component of the contract for the building contractor is remuneration. The provisions relating to payment establish the manner in which the building contractor receives money for the work/services provided and what processes must be followed. Depending on the type of contract, > Chapter Types of contracts remuneration is arranged in accordance with work done or the stage of completion, or an agreed-upon payment plan. With measurement contracts, the work/service actually provided must be listed in a verifiable invoice and documented with measured quantities.

It is possible to agree that payment is not to be made until the work/service has been completed. As a rule, however, the building contractor can submit interim/on-account invoices at appropriate intervals in order to cover the ongoing cost of the construction work and to ensure liquidity. Typical time intervals range from one month to several months. The building contractor will not submit the final invoice until after completion of all the work and services in the contract.

On-account invoices

For some building work, it can be appropriate to pay in advance. Particularly in the case of work for which the building contractor has to pay large amounts of money up front, a payment is made before the item has been procured or installed. However, usually such payment is secured by a prepayment guarantee to enable the client to secure his payment without the work having been completed. > Chapter Contractual provisions, Security

Prepayment

●

Some building contracts make provision for work on an hourly basis, in particular for work that is difficult to describe or for work that could not be anticipated at the beginning during the tender stage. This work at an hourly rate is usually documented using appropriate timesheets, which have to be approved by the person in charge of site supervision and subsequently countersigned. > Fig. 12

Work at an hourly rate

■

● **Example:** When windows are to be installed, the building contractor has to order all the materials beforehand and often pay for them immediately. In order to ensure the building contractor's liquidity, the client will, in consideration of a security, make part-payment to enable the contractor to buy the materials. Should the building contractor then fail to deliver the windows, the client can then demand repayment of the money from the provider of the security (usually a bank).

■ **Tip:** Work at an hourly rate often leads to disputes because it is difficult to check and allocate accurately. Sometimes building companies use hourly rate agreements to generate additional remuneration potential. For this reason, hourly rate work should only be agreed to in exceptional cases and should always require the prior approval of the person responsible for site supervision.

| Customer: John Smith | Any Company Ltd |
| | [details of company] |

Site: John Smith
Any Town

2-axle truck ☐   with crane ☐   3-axle truck ☐   4-axle truck ☐   twin-axle truck ☐   semi-trailer ☒

Reg. No. : MS XY 123   Driver: xxx   Date: xxx

Start _____ time   Finish _____ time   Break _____ hours   Total 1.25 hours

No.	Quantity	Material	Arrival	Departure	Point of loading
	36.9	Soil	07:15	07:45	XYZ
	30.3	Soil	08:45	09:15	XYZ
	41.8	Soil	10:10	10:25	XYZ

Name: xxx   Signature: xxx

Fig. 12: Example of a timesheet

PAYMENT

In addition to the agreement relating to remuneration, a building contract usually contains provisions for the payment of that remuneration. Once an invoice has been received, the supervising architect has to check this and then inform the client of the result of this check. The client will then make payment, provided he has no objections. > Fig. 13

Due date for payment/ payment term

The payment process can take some time, in particular when invoice items require further clarification or have to be checked in detail. For this reason, a due date for payment or a payment term is agreed to in the building contract, and the client has to settle the invoice within that period following receipt.

Early-payment discount/price reduction

Commercial clients will often negotiate tenders, > Chapter Contracting procedures which means that building contractors may agree to a price reduction or a discount for early payment. If a price reduction has been agreed to, this is applied to each item in the account or at the end of each invoice. As the name suggests, an early-payment discount is conditional upon early payment; it provides the building contractor with the advantage of receiving his payment earlier.

30

Should there be defects, the client can retain money for remedying the defects. For this purpose, he has to estimate the cost of remedying the defects and can then retain this amount and deduct it from the payment. Various arrangements may apply in this situation, depending on the legal position and/or the contract provisions; for example, in Germany it is possible to deduct twice the amount of the estimated cost of defect remedial work. If the building contractor has been overpaid in other construction projects, the client can offset these payments, depending on the contractual arrangement.

Offsetting/
defects retention

VARIATION ORDERS

The term variation order (or change order) generally refers to variations from the contractually agreed-upon building output; if the building contractor is asked to carry out something different from what is covered by the contract, it is possible that the remuneration will also change. Variation orders may be the result of the client asking for changes or

Types of
variation order

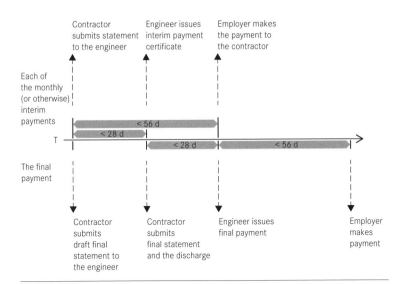

Fig. 13: Payment arrangements in the FIDIC model building contracts

○ **Note:** The payment term can vary depending on the type of invoice. In the case of interim invoices, it is usually 18 to 30 days; in the case of final invoices, a later due date can be agreed to, owing to the extensive checking required.

● **Example:** If the building contractor agrees to an early-payment discount of 3% if payment is made within ten working days, the client can reduce the payment amount by 3% from the invoice amount. If the client does not succeed in transferring the payment within the shorter payment term, he is obliged to pay the regular undiscounted invoice amount.

additions to the deliverable building work/services or may be needed when the framework conditions differ from those anticipated.

A general distinction is made between variation orders for work and those for extensions of time. Variation orders for work can be for:

— Increases or decreases in quantity (only in measurement contracts)
— Changes to the work/services
— Additional work/services
— The omission of work/services
— Work/services carried out but not ordered

Variation orders for extensions of time are issued for isolated time delays in construction that were caused not by variations in work/services, but by a third party (e.g. delays caused by the client or preceding trades) or *force majeure*.

Deliverables/
payables In view of the fact that variation orders are a regular occurrence in building projects, it is necessary to agree on contractual arrangements in order to ensure that the necessary adjustments to the contract can be made in a routine manner. A distinction must be drawn between the deliverables and the payables, because the former relates to the duty to carry out building work/services and to the respective right to instruct, while the latter relates to the resulting claims for payment, both of which
○ need to be addressed in the contract.

In the first step of a variation order, the parties must agree on what work/services the building contractor is to perform beyond the existing scope of the contract. Usually, this is linked to the work output and the defect-free completion of the building. *Defect-free completion* means that, after completion, the building must serve its intended purpose and must have been built in accordance with the recognized rules of technology. Any work/services required to achieve this usually have to be carried out by the building contractor, even if not included in the original contract.
● > Fig. 14

It is also necessary to establish to what extent the client is entitled to give binding instructions to the contractor for changing the deliverables

○ **Note:** The arrangements for adjusting the deliverables and the resulting payables are covered in detail in most model building contracts, such as the German VOB/B or the international FIDIC contracts, where there are also adequate explanatory comments. In this chapter, we therefore only cover the basic principles.

● **Example:** If the architect has forgotten to include temporary sealing in the specification for the flat roof structure and this means that a roof structure compliant with regulations is not possible, the building contractor must inform the client and, if appropriate, install the temporary sealing. The resulting remuneration is subject to a separate consideration.

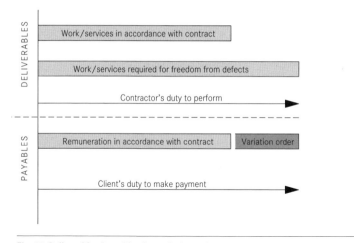

Fig. 14: Deliverables/payables for variation orders

or even the construction period. Besides the generally recognized rules of technology and the general work output, changes may also be the result of instructions from the client, e.g. asking for a different floor finish or an additional partition wall and doors for subdividing a large room.

It is customary to separately agree upon the remuneration resulting from variation orders because, in the first step, it is necessary to legally clarify whether the necessary work/service is already included in the deliverables or whether it necessitates an adjustment of the contract, which usually necessitates an adjustment to the remuneration. Either of two basic principles may apply to an adjustment to the remuneration:

Changes in remuneration

1. The adjusted price is based on the cost calculation principles used in the tender prices. For this purpose, the so-called original calculation is used: the one that the building contractor produced as the basis for his tender. Price components for the price to be computed are used on this basis. This means that the remuneration of variation orders will be at the same price level as the original tender. If the building contractor has submitted a very competitive price, the remuneration for the variation order will be just as competitive.
2. The variation order is based on current market prices. This arrangement takes into account that the building contractor may have to obtain a new tender in the market for the additional work/services, e.g. when a different material has to be installed or a different subcontractor has to be commissioned. It follows that the risk of price changes in the market is borne by the client.

Irrespective of the above, the contract may include price fluctuation clauses. Without such clauses, the building contractor has to perform at the price upon which the contract is based. However, even when a price fluctuation clause has been agreed upon, individual prices can be adjusted, for example when the price of steel changes during the course of a construction project or a new collective agreement results in higher labor costs.

ACCEPTANCE

In addition to remuneration, an important contractual duty of the client is to accept (or approve) the work output following completion. As a rule, acceptance is linked to various legal consequences. > Fig. 15

Depending on the legal situation and the provisions in the building contract, the following types of acceptance may be considered:

— Written acceptance: the client informs the building contractor in a letter about the acceptance and any defects that may still be present.
— Verbal acceptance: the client informs the building contractor personally that he accepts the work output. This is only possible in some countries, one of them being Germany, and can be problematic due to the difficulty of providing proof.
— Formal acceptance: in this case, the client and the building contractor inspect the building together. Any defects detected, and arrangements affecting the acceptance, are noted in minutes and, if appropriate, the minutes are signed by both parties.
— Acceptance committee: a committee is appointed that may consist of representatives of the contract parties, the subsequent users, and external experts. This committee inspects and checks the completed building and carries out the acceptance procedure.
— Implied acceptance: if the client behaves in a way that allows the conclusion that he approves the work output, this may be deemed to be an implied acceptance. Such implied behavior may be assumed when, for example, the client pays the final invoice without objections or retentions and moves into the building.

> ■ **Tip:** In view of the fact that, in many countries, statutory regulations take priority over model building contracts, it makes sense to deal first with the arrangements stipulated under the law. For example, in Germany the rules for acceptance are defined in Section 640 of the German Civil Code (BGB) as legally binding acceptance in contracts for work and labor. The model building contract included in VOB/B, commonly used in Germany, is of only secondary importance.

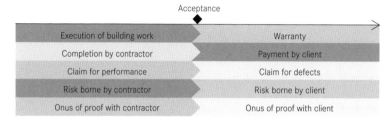

Fig. 15: Typical legal consequences of acceptance

- <u>Fictitious acceptance</u>: if the building contractor demands an acceptance procedure, he may set an appropriate period of time for the client to declare his acceptance. Should this period of time pass without a response from the client, it may be possible to infer fictitious acceptance.

The details of the acceptance procedure should be specified in the building contract, taking the legal possibilities into account. One simple option is to state that the acceptance may only be carried out formally, which means that verbal or implied acceptance cannot be claimed afterwards. However, it is also possible to agree on a more involved and step-by-step acceptance procedure. This may be appropriate, for instance, when technical installations have to undergo a trial operation to test their fault-free functioning.

The commercial acceptance between client and building contractor should not be confused with the official acceptance, in which the building control authority permits occupation of the building. The extent to which the building contractor is involved in this procedure must be defined in the contract for each case.

LIABILITY AND INSURANCE

Similar to acceptance, liability and insurance are in many cases determined by statutory regulations, which also means they are country-specific. Taking this into consideration, the allocation of risk to building contractor and client should be defined in the contract.

The starting point for allocating risk should be that each party to the contract takes on the risk for which he is inherently responsible. In situations where the client hands over to the building contractor complete architectural design documents that have been agreed upon with the specialist engineers and experts, the correctness of these documents lies in the client's risk sphere. Similarly, the freedom from defects of the building work lies in the building contractor's risk sphere. Based on these two principles, various different details can be agreed on, and the scope of risk defined or transferred to the one party or the other. It must be borne in mind, however, that transferring an unreasonably high degree of risk

Contractual arrangement

Official acceptance

Allocation of risk

to the building contractor usually results in the contractor declining to submit a tender, or adding extra amounts to the tender sum to cover the imposed risk. It is the client's task to weigh the advantage of transferring more risk against the resulting increased costs.

Contractual arrangements In order to avoid later disputes, it is important to make unequivocal arrangements in the contract regarding the allocation of risk. Some of the areas affected are:

- Any defects in the design
- Continuation of the design process
- Any risk relating to approval and official acceptance
- Quantity risk/consolidation
- Price adjustments
- Claims for defects
- Liability for each party's own defects/damage
- Liability for damage and interventions by third parties
- Limitation of liability, if any
- Defect remediation processes and claims

Insurance In addition to clarifying the position on liability, it is also important to agree on binding protection measures. In particular, this includes public liability insurance and builders' risk insurance. Taken altogether, the insurance policies must have the effect that risks resulting from the activity of the building contractor (e.g. defects, damage, or other damage caused by the work), as well as risks involving third parties, are insured.

SECURITY

Securing contractual obligations In view of the fact that the construction of a building often involves large amounts of money, contract partners often request security to reduce their own risk. This can be an instrument to secure the client's payment, which the building contractor requests because of his financial outlay and the delay between completion of the work/services and the accounts. Conversely, the client may also wish to have a security to ensure that the building contractor will follow through with his obligation to eliminate defects during the defects liability period. In the case of building contracts with a larger project volume, it is common to arrange mutual securities. Securities are most often arranged by the following measures:

- Retention of money
- Prepayments
- Provision of guarantees
- Provision of cash sums
- Collateral securities or similar

In order to provide greater security for the client, it is possible to agree that a percentage of the intermediate invoice amounts is retained until the work output has been completed. Payment of the complete amount is not due until this is the case. It is also possible to agree on retention of, for example, 5% of the final account until the end of the defects liability period in order to secure any later consequences and concealed defects. Retention of money

In order to secure payment to the building contractor, the simplest solution is to agree on prepayments so that the building contractor always has adequate liquidity for carrying out the work/services. However, reducing the building contractor's risk leads to increased risk for the client, which is usually secured in turn by a guarantee. Prepayment

Guarantees are third-party instruments that provide financial security to the contract partners. As a rule, they are provided by banks, but they can also be supplied by others, such as a parent company or an insurance company. Depending on the purpose of the guarantee, these main distinctions are made: Guarantees

— Payment guarantee: a third party guarantees that rightful claims for payment by the building contractor will be properly settled.
— Prepayment guarantee: a third party guarantees that a prepayment by the client will be repaid in the event that the underlying work/ services are not carried out by the building contractor.
— Performance guarantee: a third party guarantees that compensation will be paid for financial loss incurred by the client if the building contractor does not complete the contracted work/services. Usually this is subject to a ceiling of, say, 5–10% of the contract sum, which is intended to compensate the client for financial disadvantages resulting from having to involve a new building company.
— Warranty bond: during the guarantee period, a third party guarantees that the client will be compensated for any financial loss incurred due to defects if the building contractor does not eliminate these. Usually this is subject to a ceiling of 5% of the final account sum, which is intended to compensate the client for financial disadvantages resulting from having to involve a new building company.

● **Example:** During a storm, a site fence falls onto the road and damages a car; there must be adequate insurance protection for this situation that insures third-party risks associated with the building site. Likewise, it is possible that theft of building materials or machines leads to significant risks in terms of costs and time delays; these risks should also be covered by insurance.

It is also possible to deposit an amount of money as security in an escrow account, which cannot be withdrawn without the agreement of the contract partner.

Collateral securities

In Germany it is also possible for building contractors to enter their entitlements in the land register for the building plot as collateral security. This ensures that the building contractor can enforce his entitlement if necessary via the courts, for example, in cases where the client cannot pay due to insolvency.

Contractual arrangements

As a general rule, the building contract should include arrangements as to the chosen security. Furthermore, it is important to clarify that there is no duplication in the way individual contract interests are secured. This means, for example, that the client can make provision for a security-related retention *or* for the submission of a warranty, but cannot demand both as duplicated security.

DISPUTE RESOLUTION MECHANISMS

Potential for dispute in the building contract

It goes without saying that one should try to arrange all contract items in such a way that no disputes arise regarding the deliverables or payables. Even though it is clearly best for all parties to a contract to handle construction projects as partners, it is nevertheless common for problems to arise, again and again, due to unforeseen events or misunderstandings between the parties. In such situations, much depends on the respective personnel dealing with the project on both sides and the respective company cultures as to whether such difficulties can be resolved satisfactorily for both sides, or whether they lead to a dispute. Since, at the beginning of a project, it is usually not possible to foresee how the cooperation on the construction process will develop, and in view of the fact that the stakeholders often have to cooperate to a high degree, it is useful to include conflict resolution mechanisms in the building contract. If, at a time when both contract partners are still acting in an amicable way, the partners agree how to proceed in the case of an escalating dispute, it is generally easier to resolve any subsequent differences.

Conflict resolution procedures

Conflict resolution mechanisms can make provisions for mutual communication in a simple way and provide a structure for clarifying discussions; however, it is also possible to provide for complex decision processes involving experts or arbitration courts. The latter can be invoked by the parties to the contract in order to come to a decision where the parties are locked in an irresolvable dispute.

Courts of arbitration

The contract should contain provisions as to the composition of such courts of arbitration, and which processes and timescales are to apply to the findings of the arbitrator. For example, it is possible in the case of large projects for both parties to appoint an arbitrator, who in turn will appoint a third arbitrator in order to come to a neutral decision.

In areas without unequivocal legal determination, courts of arbitration should be given an important role in order to make the binding nature of the contract clear to both parties. It is also important to define in the contract the extent to which an arbitration award is binding for both parties and is directly executable, or whether it is possible to involve national law courts or international courts of arbitration as well. > Fig. 16

Relevance of the dispute resolution

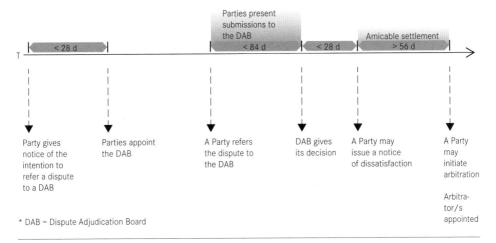

Fig. 16: Conflict resolution mechanism in international FIDIC contracts

Contract components

In addition to defining the contractual conditions addressed in the previous chapter in the building contract, the question arises as to what other components are included in a building contract. A building contract is based on various documents, such as drawings, specifications, and expert reports, that describe the project and define the framework conditions for the execution of the work. Therefore, we explain below the important components required for defining the deliverables and enabling building contractors to submit a bid in the tender process. A decision must be made in each tender procedure and for each project concerning which documents and what information will be needed by the bidder in order to enable him to clearly calculate the cost of the work/services, since these ultimately form the basis of the contract and the building work.

List of typical components of a building contract: > Fig. 17

— The building contract itself or an awarding letter
— Contractual conditions and preliminary notes
— If appropriate, a description of the building or a preamble, as definition of the work output
— Description of the work/services to be done
— The tender prices submitted by the building contractor
— Drawings, including detail drawings if applicable
— Expert/technical reports
— Patterns and samples, if applicable
— Photographic documentation, if applicable

The documents to be included may vary significantly, depending on what stage the design process has reached when the contract is awarded, and depending on the type of contract.

Order of precedence   An order of precedence should be agreed upon in the contract; this determines the order in which the components of the contract are applicable. This can be important when there are contradictions or conflicts
● between different contract components.

> ● **Example:** A drawing shows that a canopy is to be constructed using a 120 mm high galvanized steel profile. However, the narrative in the specifications states a profile height of 80 mm, and the preliminary notes say that all steel components are only to be primed. The question here is which information takes precedence.

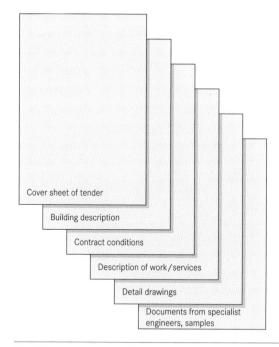

Fig. 17: Components of a building contract

A typical order of precedence could be as follows:

1. Building contract
2. Minutes of contract negotiations, including clarifications
3. Description of work/services
4. Drawings
5. Room schedule
6. Expert fire protection report, etc.
7. Project-specific contract conditions
8. Building contractor's tender
9. Generally applicable contract conditions
10. Technical standards

The exact order of precedence of the individual elements is then determined for each specific project. A typical approach is to place components with a direct reference to the project, or detailed content, ahead of generally applicable components. The question of whether the contractor's tender should take lower priority than all the client's documents must be clarified for each project, particularly in view of any limitations or modifications of the deliverables included in the tender.

It is also important to clarify which general technical standards are to be complied with. As a rule, this is done by specifying these standards in the contract, unless this is regulated by general public instruments, as in Germany. Almost all countries have regulatory instruments and standards that can be used as a basis for building contracts. Unless the contract states otherwise, standards and other regulatory instruments should always have a lower priority than the project-specific documents, such as drawings and descriptions of work/services.

Where general standards apply that must always be complied with in a certain country, these are referred to as "generally recognized rules of technology."

DESCRIPTION OF WORK/SERVICES

The core of each building contract consists of the description of work/services, which contains a definition of the intended work output. Such descriptions are produced by the architects and are handed over to potential bidders as part of the tender documents; based on these descriptions, the bidders will calculate the costs for their tender submission. Essentially, the description of work/services defines the deliverables of the building contract.

The work/services can be described either in detailed specifications or by defining the desired functions of the building. To some extent, this also has an effect on the choice of tendering procedure and type of building contract (measurement contract or lump sum contract). > Chapter Types of contracts

The two different types of contracts use different ways of describing the work:

— Specifications
— Functional description of work/services (work schedule)

Specifications describe the work/services to be rendered in detail as individual items. These items consist of an ordinal number, a short and a long text, an item type, and the quantity. In addition, there are spaces

○ **Note:** Generally recognized rules of technology are considered to be all regulatory instruments that have been considered to be correct by the relevant professional bodies and that have also been established in practice. This means that the generally recognized rules of technology are not limited to standards and laws, but also include manufacturer and installation instructions, recommendations by associations, notes and guidelines from professional institutes, and so on

■ **Tip:** In the "Basics" book titled *Tendering*, Tim Brandt and Sebastian Franssen cover in detail how to produce specifications and work schedules.

```
2. Interior fit-out/finishing
   2.1 Drywalling work
      2.1.4 Sheetrock walls, 125 mm                          Quantity      Unit price        Total price
            Sheetrock wall, metal studs, alu-C profiles,
            lined on both sides (each 2 × 12.5 mm sheetrock board),
            60 mm gap filled with mineral wool, skimmed and
            sanded (Q3)
            Height: 2.85 m
            Product designation: XXX (or equivalent)
            If different product, state make:

            _____    82 m²      _____        _____


      2.1.5 Sheetrock walls, 200 mm
            Sheetrock wall, metal studs, alu-C profiles,
            lined on both sides (each 2 × 12.5 mm sheetrock board),
            100 mm gap filled with mineral wool, skimmed and
            sanded (Q2)
            Height: 2.85 m
            Product designation: XXX (or equivalent)
            If different product, state make:

            _____    65 m²      _____        _____


      2.1.6 Suspended sheetrock ceiling
            Sheetrock ceiling, suspended (180 mm below
            concrete slab), aluminum suspension substructure
            80 mm mineral wool for sound absorption
            Product designation: XXX (or equivalent)
            If different product, state make:

            _____    253 m²     _____        _____
```

Fig. 18: Example of items in specifications

for the tender prices of the building contractor, where the price per unit and the stated quantity are to be entered. > Fig. 18

Specifications can be laid out to accompany measurement contracts or detailed lump sum contracts.

The work schedule or functional description of work/services does not usually describe the exact method of carrying out the work, but is confined to determining the result and objective of the work. The building contractor can therefore decide on the basis of his professional knowledge and competence how to achieve that objective, and determine the best possible methods for achieving it.

Functional descriptions of work/services can vary a great deal, depending on the degree of detail. If the contract is awarded at the beginning of the design process, it usually only includes descriptions of the building and lists of room requirements, without additional design

Work schedule

documents. Where a design has been produced, room schedules or descriptions of the building components or trades/component groups may be used in order to define the objectives of the project. > Fig. 19

Specifications can be laid out to accompany measurement contracts or detailed lump sum contracts. Work schedules and/or functional descriptions of work/services are usually used in combination with global lump sum contracts.

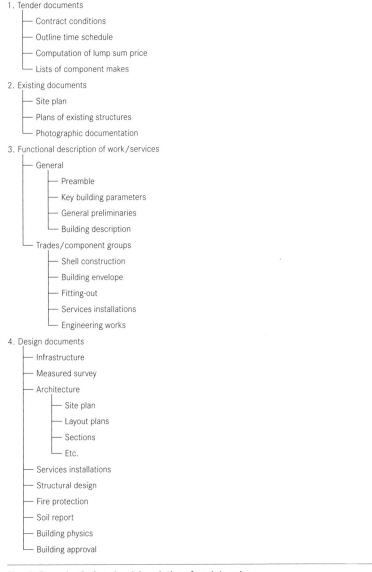

1. Tender documents
    ├── Contract conditions
    ├── Outline time schedule
    ├── Computation of lump sum price
    └── Lists of component makes
2. Existing documents
    ├── Site plan
    ├── Plans of existing structures
    └── Photographic documentation
3. Functional description of work/services
    ├── General
    │   ├── Preamble
    │   ├── Key building parameters
    │   ├── General preliminaries
    │   └── Building description
    └── Trades/component groups
         ├── Shell construction
         ├── Building envelope
         ├── Fitting-out
         ├── Services installations
         └── Engineering works
4. Design documents
    ├── Infrastructure
    ├── Measured survey
    ├── Architecture
    │   ├── Site plan
    │   ├── Layout plans
    │   ├── Sections
    │   └── Etc.
    ├── Services installations
    ├── Structural design
    ├── Fire protection
    ├── Soil report
    ├── Building physics
    └── Building approval

Fig. 19: **Example of a functional description of work/services**

DESIGN DOCUMENTS, EXPERT REPORTS

In addition to the narrative included in the description of work and Design documents services, the building contractor needs design documents that show the layout and dimensions of the work to be carried out. Depending on when the contract is awarded, different design stages will form the basis of the building contract:

— Contract awarded with outline design drawings > Fig. 20
— Contract awarded with schematic design drawings ready for approval or approved > Fig. 21
— Contract awarded with advanced schematic design drawings and key details
— Contract awarded with fully completed detailed design drawings
   > Fig. 22

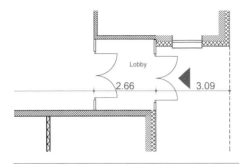

Fig. 20: Level of detail provided in outline design (section of drawing)

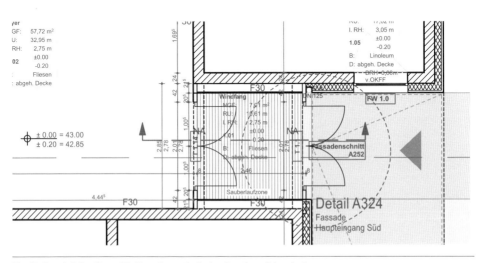

Fig. 21: Level of detail provided in schematic design (section of drawing)

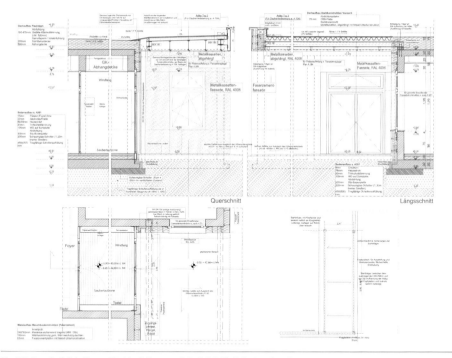

Querschnitt

Längsschnitt

Fig. 22: Level of detail provided in fully completed detailed design drawings

In cases where the building contractor does not receive completed detailed design drawings, he will have to produce these himself and include this service in the tender. > Chapter Types of contracts, Awarding contracts to general contractors

Final detailed drawings

Where final detailed drawings are produced and individual tradespeople are appointed, it may be necessary to produce specific design documents for the various trades/component groups. The building contractor should be given, at the very least, the following plans as a project overview:

— Site plan/site mobilization plan
— Layouts
— Cross-sections
— Elevations

When a project is awarded to a general contractor based on the description of the building work and services, it is customary to also include various overview plans that show the location of various components, as well as the materials and qualities. This is important in defining the required work output, since the functional description does not include the quantities of the respective items. > Figs. 23 and 24

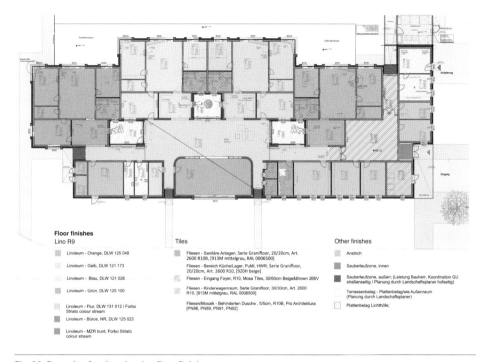

Floor finishes

Lino R9

- Linoleum - Orange, DLW 125 048
- Linoleum - Gelb, DLW 121 173
- Linoleum - Blau, DLW 121 026
- Linoleum - Grün, DLW 125 100
- Linoleum - Flur, DLW 131 012 / Forbo Striato colour stream
- Linoleum - Büros, NR, DLW 125 023
- Linoleum - MZR bunt, Forbo Striato colour stream

Tiles

- Fliesen - Sanitäre Anlagen, Serie Granifloor, 20/20cm, Art. 2600 R10B, [913M mittelgrau, RAL 0006500]
- Fliesen - Bereich Küche/Lager, PuMi, HWR, Serie Granifloor, 20/20cm, Art. 2600 R10, [920H beige]
- Fliesen - Eingang Foyer, R10, Mosa Tiles, 30/60cm Beige&Brown 266V
- Fliesen - Kinderwagenraum, Serie Granifloor, 30/30cm, Art. 2600 R10, [913M mittelgrau, RAL 0006500]
- Fliesen/Mosaik - Behinderten Dusche , 5/5cm, R10B, Pro Architektura [PN86, PN89, PN91, PN92]

Other finishes

- Anstrich
- Sauberlaufzone, innen
- Sauberlaufzone, außen; (Leistung Bauherr, Koordination GU straßenseitig / Planung durch Landschaftsplaner hofseitig)
- Terrassenbelag - Plattenbelag/wie Außenraum (Planung durch Landschaftsplaner)
- Plattenbelag Lichthöfe;

Fig. 23: Example of a plan showing floor finishes

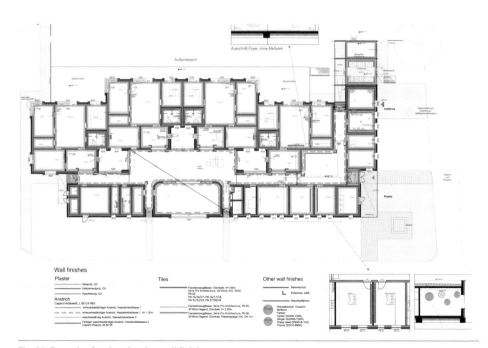

Wall finishes

Plaster

- Gipsputz, Q3
- Kalkzementputz, Q3
- Spachtelung, Q3

Anstrich

Caparol Antiwalli, L 95 C4 H92

- scheuerbeständiger Anstrich, Nassabriebsklasse 1
- scheuerbeständiger Anstrich, Nassabriebsklasse 1, HH 1,30m
- waschbeständig Anstrich, Nassabriebsklasse 3
- Fertiger waschbeständiger Anstrich, Nassabriebsklasse 3 Caparol Picazzo 45,50,55

Tiles

- Feinsteinzeugfliesen, Dünnbett, l=1,50m Serie Pro Architectura, 10/10cm, Art. 3201] PN 00 PN 25/26/27, PN 16/17/18, PN 31/32/33, PN 37/38/39
- Feinsteinzeugfliesen, Serie Pro Architectura, PN 00, 30*90cm liegend, Dünnbett, h=2,00m
- Feinsteinzeugfliesen, Serie Pro Architectura, PN 00, 30*90cm liegend, Dünnbett, Fliesenspiegel (UK, OK, h=)

Other wall finishes

- Rammschutz
- Eckschutz, weiß
- Absorberflächen
- Wandabsorber Ecophon 60/60cm Farben: Oyster (54005-Y20R) Ginger (52000S-Y30R) Poppy seed (53020-B-10G) Thyme (52010-B90G)

Fig. 24: Example of a plan showing wall finishes

47

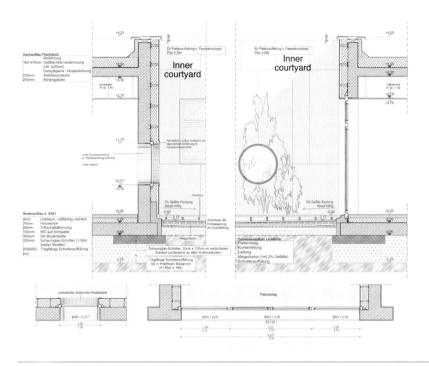

Fig. 25: Example of drawing for facade contractor

Additional plans may be provided for various trades, as required.
> Figs. 25 and 26 These could include:

— Shell construction: building pit/excavation, foundations, formwork
plans, reinforcement plans, connection details, etc.
— Windows/facade: window details, facade sections, window/door
schedules, installation plans if necessary, etc.
— Roofing and flashing work: plan view of roof, roof details, services
plans for ventilation/pipe outlets, roof drainage scheme, etc.
— Screed: installation plans for screed, floor construction details,
floor connection details
— Tiles: tile layouts, sanitary room plans, details

Expert reports In addition to design documents, many building contracts also include expert or technical reports. These may cover:

— Calculations to prove the structural integrity (structural calculations)
— Expert soil report
— Evidence of thermal insulation
— Evidence of sound insulation

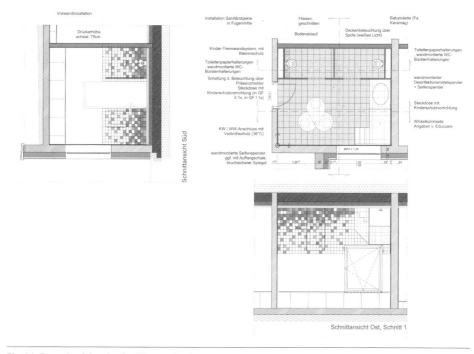

Fig. 26: Example of drawing for tiling contractor

- Fire protection concept
- If relevant, pollution analysis of existing ground and/or building

Which expert reports are included in which contracts depends on whether the respective content is relevant for the particular trade and whether the content has already been fully covered by the respective description of work and services. In order to avoid redundant documentation, expert reports should primarily be included in the contract when they are needed for better understanding and clarification of the desired work output.

OTHER COMPONENTS

Sometimes other documents are needed to clarify the desired work output or the circumstances pertaining to the project. These may cover additional information from the building control authority (building approval, drainage approval, conditions for connecting services, etc.) or other limitations or information on the building site or project.

In view of the fact that one cannot normally expect the building contractor to have visited the site prior to tendering his bid, it is usual to include photographic documentation of the construction site in the tender documents. This means that it becomes part of the contract, because the

Photographic documentation

cost calculation is partly based on this information. Photographic documentation helps bidders understand the conditions on site, the status of the site, and, sometimes, to better clarify the scope of their planned work.

● Lists of component makes or brands

If the client wants to receive information on the make or brand of components included in the tender or to specify these makes, they can either be listed directly in the description of work and services, or the contractor can be asked to state the proposed makes, or produce a list of component makes. This makes it possible to specify the quality and materials that have to be used for the project. > Tab. 2

Samples

It is also sometimes helpful to include samples or photographs of items. For example, in listed building projects, this is a convenient way of specifying surfaces and materials that must be matched with the new work. Where materials have to be installed by different trades (for example, wood veneer by the door contractor, joiner, and media engineer) it may be useful to include small sample pieces in order to ensure that all contractors can exactly match the desired finish.

Tab. 2: Example of a list of component makes

Trade/functional description	Work/building component	Preferred make	Make offered by bidder	Enclosure by bidder in the case of deviating makes
Shell construction				
3.2.4 Shell construction	Steel work/reinforcement cages	xyz		
Fassade				
3.3.1 Roof sealing/flashing	Roof sealing/flashing	xyz		
3.3.1 Roof sealing/flashing	Sloping roof insulation	xyz		
3.3.1 Roof sealing/flashing	Roof drainage inlets	xyz		
3.3.2 Curtain wall facade	Fiber cement board	xyz		
3.3.3 External windows	Individual wood/aluminum windows; wood/aluminum window elements with integrated balcony doors	xyz		
3.3.3 External windows	Window handles/hand levers	xyz		
3.3.4 Solar screening	Retractable blind system for box-type windows and curtain wall facade	xyz		
Fitting-out/finishing				
....	....	....		

● **Example:** A painter/decorator has been asked to close the joints in prefabricated component walls. It helps to take a photograph of the joints, including a folding rule for scale, so that the size and depth of the joints can be judged. For a dry-lining contractor who has to calculate the cost of a suspended ceiling, it is useful to see a photograph of the ceiling showing its services installations.

Contracting procedures

The main provisions and components of the building contract have been explained in the previous chapters. We will now look at how a building contract is selected, and which contractual aspects have to be taken into consideration when undertaking a building project.

OBJECTIVES AND PRINCIPLES

At the beginning of a design project, important milestones such as the date of contract award should be clarified as part of the design process. This makes it possible to conclude suitable agreements with the architects and specialist engineers covering the necessary scope of work. Likewise, the decision as to whether contracts for the building work are to be awarded to individual trades or to a general contractor should be made at an early stage in the design process so that the content of the designs and the tender documents can be planned appropriately. Once these decisions have been made, it is possible to select a suitable type of contract, the advantages and disadvantages of which have to be weighed up for each respective project.

Decisions at the beginning of the project

Once the time of contract award and the type of contract have been determined, a decision needs to be made as to the form of the building contract and the degree of detail that will be included. Country-specific and international model contracts, as well as general contract conditions, are available that can be used as a basis for devising a contract. > Appendix, Model contracts

Devising a contract on the basis of model contracts

However, it is not advisable to adopt general regulatory instruments without examination and adaptation to the respective project. Model contracts are deliberately formulated to be suitable for the widest possible range of building types, project sizes, and execution methods; they do not as a rule contain specific provisions. This means that specific content has to be adjusted or supplemented to suit the respective situation in order to produce a good building contract based on the model contract. ∎

> ∎ **Tip:** Public clients are often obliged to use certain model contracts and can modify these only under certain conditions. In this case, it is necessary to discuss with the public client what options are available for detailing and supplementing project-specific content.

General terms and conditions

Many professional clients, such as property companies or corporations, have their own contract conditions that they want included in the building contract as general terms and conditions. These may be formulated to cover all procurement activities throughout the company, or specifically building procurement. Where general terms and conditions are stipulated by the client, they have to be analyzed in order to establish what content is already covered and what has to be added.

Individual building contracts

At times it is appropriate to develop complete individual contracts for a project. In particular, this should be considered when it is not possible to draw up a straightforward contract for large, complex, or special projects, or when the intention is to involve the bidder in the setting up of the contract. In this case, it is advisable to involve a specialized lawyer. Individual building contracts have the significant advantage that they can be fully designed for the requirements of the project and to suit those involved in the contract. On the other hand, however, there is a chance that omissions or clauses that are too general in these contracts may lead to unforeseen risks because, in contrast to the clauses in generally applicable model contracts, some of the provisions will not have been tested and clarified in their meaning on the basis of previous court judgments.

Building contracts stipulated by the client

Many clients include finalized building contracts when they send out tender documents and bidders have only limited scope for modifying these contracts. The advantage is that bidders are already informed about all framework conditions when they prepare their cost calculation. A disadvantage is, however, that bidders may not submit a tender because of clauses in the contract that are not acceptable to them even though, from the client's point of view, these clauses might have been negotiable.

Bidders involved in negotiating contracts

Another approach is to negotiate contracts directly with the preferred bidder or bidders. One option is to include model contracts in the tender documents as a basis for negotiation; alternatively, the contract may be individually negotiated in the context of an award meeting following the submission of tenders. This has the advantage that both contract parties can make their preferences known and mutually agree on the contract conditions. It is important to remember, though, that the respective

○ **Note:** General terms and conditions (GTC) are contract provisions that have been established as the business principles of a party to the contract and do not just relate to a single project. Depending on the legal situation in the country, GTC must comply with specific rules. For example, in Germany, GTC must not include any clauses that impose an uncommon risk on another contract party.

tenders are only conditionally binding in this instance, because the building contractor was not able to take the contract provisions into account when producing the cost calculation.

A reasonable approach is determined by the client's wish to negotiate these conditions as well as whether he is, in fact, allowed to do so, and to what extent the client wants to transfer risks to the building contractor or negotiate these fairly with him.

How to handle contract risks

In situations where the building contractor is expected to take on all risks one-sidedly, it is possible, in times of a strong market, that building contractors may withdraw from the tender procedure or that they may reflect the risks with significant increases in the tender prices. On the other hand, this may be the better alternative for the client, for example, when a fixed budget must not be exceeded.

As a general principle, it makes sense for the client to take a reasonable approach in the transfer of risks. In some countries (e.g. Germany) it is even prohibited by law to transfer unreasonable risks. This is based on the following principle: those who are in charge of the design/detailing of a process should also bear the risk for this process. This ensures that the party responsible for the design of the process and who has the best detailed knowledge of this process must take responsibility for its correctness. In other countries, such as the United Kingdom, this protection is only provided for private individuals; in the case of contracts between commercial entities, only the text of the contract is relevant, which means that it is possible to fully transfer risks.

In any case, contracts should always contain very clear provisions as to the allocation of the respective risks.

PROCEDURE LEADING TO AWARDING A CONTRACT

Before a building contract is concluded it is usually necessary to engage in an award procedure in order to obtain sufficiently comparable tenders and to be able to select the best bidder. Public clients are usually bound by set procedures that specify the various steps that have to be completed. Private clients are free to choose the steps of this procedure, even though, as a rule, these are similar if somewhat less regimented. > Fig. 27

An essential component of an awarding process is the compilation of all tender documents on the client side. As a minimum requirement, this normally involves the following documents:

Producing tender documents

—   Covering letter
—   Contract conditions and, if appropriate, a model contract
—   Preliminary notes/description of framework conditions
—   Description of work and services
—   Drawings
—   Expert reports

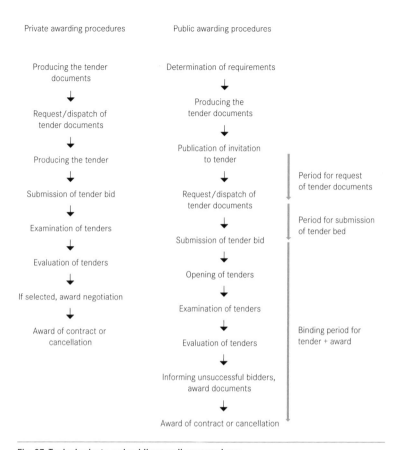

Private awarding procedures

Producing the tender documents
↓
Request/dispatch of tender documents
↓
Producing the tender
↓
Submission of tender bid
↓
Examination of tenders
↓
Evaluation of tenders
↓
If selected, award negotiation
↓
Award of contract or cancellation

Public awarding procedures

Determination of requirements
↓
Producing the tender documents
↓
Publication of invitation to tender
↓
Request/dispatch of tender documents
↓
Submission of tender bid
↓
Opening of tenders
↓
Examination of tenders
↓
Evaluation of tenders
↓
Informing unsuccessful bidders, award documents
↓
Award of contract or cancellation

Period for request of tender documents

Period for submission of tender bed

Binding period for tender + award

Fig. 27: Typical private and public awarding procedures

The objective of this compilation is to include all information on work and services directly or indirectly required for execution of the building, and thereby to enable all bidders to produce comparable tenders.

Public notice   In the case of public clients, it may be a requirement to publicly announce that a request for tenders will be forthcoming. When the request for tenders is published directly, the publication must be designed to reach as many potential bidders as possible. It is often in the interest of private clients as well to notify potential bidders before the actual request for tender is made.

Dispatch of documents   Depending on the procedure, the request for tenders may be either published on an internet website or sent by mail. In many cases, a time period is set in which building contractors can apply to be considered. It is important for all bidders to be in possession of the information at the same time so as not to create any advantage or disadvantage.

The building contractors are given a set time period within which the tenders have to be produced. This time period should not be too short, so that bidders have the opportunity to study and deal with the contract documents in depth. As a general principle, this tender period should not be less than two weeks; in the case of larger or more complex projects for which bidders may have to obtain prices from subcontractors or for special materials, at least four weeks should be allowed.

The tender period ends with the submission of the tenders (tendering of the bids) on the submission date; on that date, all tenders are opened and any tenders received beforehand are kept closed until that date. In the case of public clients, this follows a specific procedure in order to prevent any exertion of influence. In the case of private clients, a decision must be made as to whether tenders are to be submitted to the client or directly to the consulting architect.

Once the tenders have been opened, they must be examined and evaluated. Typical points of examination are:

— Completeness of the tender
— Restrictions or informative notes from the bidder
— Examination for calculation errors
— Appropriateness of prices
— Financial standing and competence of bidder
— Comparison of bidders

On the basis of the evaluation of tenders, an award proposal is produced and submitted to the client.

Depending on the type of client and the respective requirements, a building contractor will then be awarded the contract directly or preliminary discussions or award negotiations will be carried out. In view of the fact that public clients are not usually allowed to negotiate the price, building contractors are often awarded the contract directly. Where certain items require clarification, it is possible to carry out clarification discussions. Private clients will often invite the successful bidder or bidders to attend award negotiations in which the price, the contract, certain provisions, execution dates, etc. are negotiated. These award negotiations have the purpose of getting to know the potential contract partner and, in certain situations, of enabling the client to negotiate additional requirements. > Chapter Contracting procedures, Objectives and principles

Once the bidder who is to carry out the building work/services has been selected, a building contract must be concluded with him. In the case of public clients, the conditions of the contract are sometimes included in the tender documents so that when a bidder has been selected, the order is placed with him by a letter of appointment. In the standard situation, however, both parties to the contract will sign the building contract, either in the original form or in the form finalized in the contract negotiations.

Tender period

Submission

Evaluation of tenders

Contract award negotiation

Placing the contract

Depositing the original cost calculation and guarantee

When a building contractor is awarded the contract and a building contract is signed, it is usual for the building contractor to have to provide further documents to the client. These may include no objection certificates, the sealed original calculation, and guarantees. > Chapter Contractual provisions, Security The original cost calculation is deposited sealed as proof of the cost calculation at the time of submitting the tender. The unit prices stated in the cost calculation will be used for the purpose of pricing variation orders.

MEASURES ASSOCIATED WITH THE BUILDING WORK

Once a contract has been concluded, the building contractor will start with his preparatory work, such as producing additional designs, ordering materials, work preparation, capacity planning, etc. and will then start with the actual construction work. While construction work is in progress it is usually necessary to check, and if necessary request, that the contract provisions are properly complied with. This involves various processes and work levels. > Figs. 28 and 29

Coordination of work

Where contracts are awarded to several bidders, the client's supervisor is responsible for coordinating the different building contractors. > Chapter Types of contracts, Awarding contracts to individual trades For this purpose, a coordination time schedule is produced and there will be site meetings

■ at regular intervals.

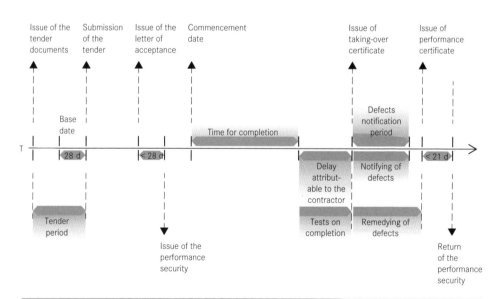

Fig. 28: Typical construction process in accordance with FIDIC

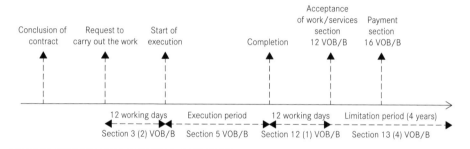

Fig. 29: Typical construction process in accordance with VOB/B

Checking the quality of the work is an important task. The finished work must comply with the contractual requirements as defined in the description of work/services, the design documents, and the expert reports. These include concrete information and descriptions of quality that must be complied with. In addition, there will be references to general standards, such as those included in regulations, standards, and manufacturer and installation guidelines, which must also be complied with. These generally recognized rules of technology are the foundation for assuring the quality of the building work; on that basis, only specific requirements have to be set out in detail. > Chapter Contract components Having said that, it may actually be easier to check specific elements of the description of work/services while work is in progress than to rely on general standards, since this would involve extensive background knowledge as to what quality must be provided by building contractors in the context of the generally recognized rules of technology.

Checking the quality

Another important supervisory function is to deal with the contract conditions mentioned in the Chapters Contractual provisions, Remuneration, and Payment. In addition to the verification of the invoices by the supervising architect and payment by the client, it is also necessary to produce cost updates to keep the client informed about the up-to-date cost situation of his project. Once an invoice has been verified, an invoice verification sheet is produced, which shows the status of performance and remuneration and all other conditions, such as discounts, early

Accounts and payment

■ **Tip:** The activities involved in supervising a construction project are described in detail in *Basics Site Management* by Lars-Phillip Rusch. Time scheduling is covered by the "Basics" volume *Construction Scheduling* by Bert Bielefeld.

payment discounts, and retentions. > Fig. 30 A cost overview has to be produced at regular intervals covering all trades/component groups to enable the client to take the necessary action in the case of any deviations from the budget.

Invoice verification
(cumulative invoice verification)   1. Ref. any company

Client	Client XXX	Part of building:		
Project	E.g. demolition work			
Contract No.:	12345	Project No.:	12345	Cost center: XY
Titel:		No.:		Contractor: Any company

Date received:	xx.xx.xx	Invoice date:	xx.xx.xx	Invoice No.: 12345
Verifiable?	☒ Yes ☐ No	Reason:		
	☐ Verifiable from date/reason			

	Without VAT €	VAT 19% €	With VAT €
1. Amount prior to verification	200,000.00		
2. Amount verified before discounts	200,000.00		
3. Discounts 3%	6,000.00		
4. Net amount	194,000.00		
5. Retention ☐ 5% ☒ 10%	(-) 19,400.00		
6. Amount	174,600.00		
7. Amount(s) paid to date	(-) 120,000.00		
8. Outstanding balance	54,600.00		
9. Deductions/charges as per enclosure	(-)		
10. Outstanding balance (payable)	54,600.00		
11. Early payment discount 0.00%			
12. Amount payable	54,600.00	10,374.00	64,974.00

Comments

The amount invoiced is covered by the work carried out to date.

Validity	checked:	
Calculations	checked:	
Released for payment:		

Fig. 30: Typical invoice verification sheet

Once the building work or certain parts thereof have been completed, the building contractor can make a request for an acceptance or partial acceptance procedure. By accepting the work, the client confirms his basic agreement and that the work is essentially free from defects. In most cases the building contract contains provisions for the handover procedure. > Chapter Contractual provisions, Acceptance

Acceptance/ handover

This means that the actions to be carried out by the supervising officer are specified in the contractual provisions. In the case of a formal acceptance procedure, the supervising officer will carry out the technical examination of the building work and will undertake a joint inspection with the client and the building contractor in order to arrive at an assessment. From a legal point of view, it is the client who accepts the building work; the supervising officer provides the client with the necessary information to enable him to assess the completed building work, as the client himself may not have the necessary detailed knowledge.

The act of acceptance has certain legal consequences. One of them is that the fulfillment stage ends and the defects liability period begins. It also means that, after acceptance, the building contractor is no longer obliged to carry out additional work at contract prices. Furthermore, any risk associated with the building, such as the risk of damage, passes to the client; this means that it is in the building contractor's interest to obtain acceptance as quickly as possible, particularly as far as fragile components such as windows and doors are concerned. For this reason, building contractors will sometimes ask for partial acceptance or so-called "visual acceptance," during which the fitted or installed components are jointly inspected and assessed.

If defects are detected during the acceptance procedure or they occur during the defects liability period owing to mistakes made by the building contractor, the building contractor has a duty to eliminate these. It is therefore important, during the acceptance procedure, to list all detectable defects exactly with a date for eliminating them so as not to invalidate any claims against building contractors. In addition, the supervising officer has to coordinate and monitor the elimination of defects. As a rule, the building contractor will notify the client when the defects have been eliminated.

Elimination of defects

Depending on the contractual provisions, further work may have to be carried out during the defects liability period. This can involve a commissioning period during which the client or user of the building undertakes the commissioning and maintenance of installations, along with the building contractor. In the case of complex installations, it is also possible to agree that the building contractor will commission the plant and installations and operate these for a certain period of time before the client takes over the fully functioning and commissioned installation.

Defects liability period

If the building contract does not include any additional work or performance guarantees after acceptance, the building contractor's obligation is limited to the elimination of any occurring defects that are due to defective performance during the construction period.

During the defects liability period, the building contractor has to provide a security in the form of a guarantee or monies retained by the client, depending on the respective contractual provision; the purpose of this is to provide the client with financial security for the elimination of any defects. > Chapter Contractual provisions, Security These securities are returned to the building contractor at the end of the defects liability period.

DOCUMENTATION

All important steps of the design and construction process, as well as the final result, must be documented.

This provides the necessary transparency of the process to all stakeholders, and information to the client. For example, usually the client/his project manager wants to be regularly informed about the progress of the project and any problems in order to be able to make decisions while work is still in progress and, if necessary, to adjust the objectives of the project.

Furthermore, the documentation is used to provide evidence in the case of future claims by one party to the contract or the other. It is possible for disagreements to arise in the course of a project, such as over the finished quality, payments, or similar matters which, as a last resort, have to be resolved by the courts. It is prudent and necessary to create good documentary evidence as a basis of defense against unreasonable claims.

A distinction is made between different types of documentation:

- Documentation in the field of project management
- Design process documentation
- Site supervision documentation during the construction phase
- Building contractor's documentation during the construction phase
- Final project documentation

From the perspective of the building contract, the last three points are of particular importance. During the construction phase, both the supervising officer and the building contractor will produce documentary evidence of the construction process. For example, the supervising officer, on behalf of the client, monitors and documents the construction progress in a log book, the coordination of building contractors (e.g. in the minutes of site meetings), the correspondence with the client's contract partners, any changes in the cost budget, and any defects in the finished quality in defects lists; it is also possible to have an expert involved for this purpose. The building contractor will keep daily reports on work and events, take measurements of quantities, or continue the cost calculation following the awarding of the contract. Which of these documents are made available to the other party to the contract is normally stated in the building contract. In many building contracts the building contractors are obligated to submit daily and weekly reports at regular intervals.

Similarly, general contractors are often obligated to provide the client with a monthly update of the construction time schedule.

The building contract usually includes provisions about what final documentation must be submitted by the building contractor as part of the acceptance procedure. This includes all documents required for providing evidence of the quality and for the ongoing use of the building. Evidence of quality may be provided in the form of specialist contractor certificates on the correct completion, expert/technical reports, or a design "as built" that shows the actual status as built. Final documentation by the building contractor

In order to ensure that the client can competently operate his building/s, the respective operating instructions, care and maintenance instructions, and product specifications must be compiled for all technical components and installations. This means that, when the property is handed over, inductions have to be carried out to explain to future users, for instance, how to operate ventilation systems or items of building automation.

Depending on the size of the project and the level of professionalism of the client, the building contract will contain more or less exact arrangements as to what documents must be included in the final documentation and how these are to be prepared.

The supervising officer, acting on behalf of the client, will produce final documentation that is handed to the client. This is mainly based on the documents provided by the various contractors involved in the project. In addition, there are final reports or document compilations from the construction phase. For example, comprehensive project documentation may include the following: Final documentation produced by the supervising officer

— Signed building contracts
— Amendments, instructions
— Remuneration, payments
— Variation/change orders
— Information on deadlines
— Correspondence, minutes
— Defects lists and notices of defect elimination
— Acceptance minutes
— Photographic documentation
— Defects liability periods
— Security instruments

At the end of a construction process the supervising officer has the duty to request and compile all documents from the executing building contractors; this may require a considerable effort since the volume of documents is always growing. The main reason for this is that larger buildings involve ever greater amounts of technical installations and automated mechanisms, and that clients want to operate their buildings ever more efficiently using professional facilities management.

Conclusion

Building contracts are an important element in the work of architects and engineers because, generally speaking, all design activities are intended to end up with a completed building. The interaction and cooperation of the designing and executing professions is essential to the success of a project. And finally, every project needs clear budgets and completion dates.

In order to be able to successfully support projects from the initial design idea to ultimate completion, it is important for architects and engineers to understand and sensibly apply the standard practices for erecting buildings. In many projects, existing model contracts are used as the basis for commissioning building contractors. It is still necessary, however, to understand the control mechanisms and the options for describing work and services and to define these in a binding way.

Some typical model contracts are listed in the appendix. This book intentionally only covers the general control mechanisms in order to develop awareness in budding architects, rather than to encourage them to just be users of pre-drafted contracts. As a rule, the detailed drafting of building contracts or the adaptation of model contracts is undertaken by lawyers, but the overall coordination and control of the process is the task of architects. For architects it is also important that they understand the contribution made by the various specialist disciplines, such as structural engineering, building physics, or technical services engineering, even if they themselves are not capable of providing the respective services. The aim of this "Basics" volume is to enable readers to produce building contracts in cooperation with lawyers and to successfully complete projects.

Appendix

MODEL CONTRACTS

The list below contains some model contracts, some that are used in specific countries and some that are established internationally.

Model building contract	Scope of application
FIDIC	International
NEC3/ECC	United Kingdom/international
CPC 2013	United Kingdom/international
ECE	United Kingdom/international
AIA	USA
Orgalime	Plant engineering (international)
VOB/B	Germany
Austrian Standard Ö-Norm B2110	Austria
Swiss Standard SIA-Norm 118	Switzerland
CCAG travaux	France (public)
NF P 03-001	France (private)

LITERATURE

John Adriaanse: *Construction Contract Law*, Kindle Edition, Palgrave, London/New York 2016

Ellis Baker, Ben Mellors, Scott Chalmers, Anthony Lavers: *FIDIC Contracts—Law and Practice*, Informa, London 2013

Bert Bielefeld (Ed.): *Basics Project Management Architecture*, Birkhäuser, Basel 2013

Bert Bielefeld: *Basics Construction Scheduling*, Birkhäuser, Basel 2007

Bert Bielefeld, Roland Schneider: *Basics Budgeting*, Birkhäuser, Basel 2007

Tim Brandt, Sebastian Franssen: *Basics Tendering*, Birkhäuser, Basel 2007

DIN e.V., DVA (Ed.): *VOB 2016 in English: German Construction Contract Procedures: Parts A, B and C*, Beuth, Berlin 2017

Jim Mason: *Construction Law—From Beginner to Practitioner*, Routledge, Abingdon/New York 2016

Lukas Klee: *International Construction Contract Law*, Wiley Blackwell, Chichester 2014

Hartmut Klein, *Basics Project Planning*, Birkhäuser, Basel 2007

Lars-Philipp Rusch: *Basics Site Management*, Birkhäuser, Basel 2017

ALSO AVAILABLE FROM BIRKHÄUSER:

Design

Basics Office Design
Bert Bielefeld
ISBN 978-3-0356-1382-7

Basics Barrier-free Planning
Isabella Skiba, Rahel Züger
ISBN 978-3-0356-1606-4

Basics Design and Living
Jan Krebs
ISBN 978-3-0356-1663-7

Basics Design Ideas
Bert Bielefeld,
Sebastian El Khouli
ISBN 978-3-7643-8112-7

Basics Design Methods
Kari Jormakka
ISBN 978-3-7643-8463-0

Basics Materials
M. Hegger, H. Drexler, M. Zeumer
ISBN 978-3-7643-7685-7

Basics Spatial Design
Ulrich Exner, Dietrich Pressel
ISBN 978-3-7643-8848-5

Available as a compendium:
Basics Architectural Design
Bert Bielefeld (ed.)
ISBN 978-3-03821-560-8

Fundamentals of Presentation

Basics Detail Drawing
Björn Vierhaus
ISBN 978-3-0356-1379-7

Basics Architectural Photography
Michael Heinrich
ISBN 978-3-7643-8666-5

Basics CAD
Jan Krebs
ISBN 978-3-7643-8109-7

Basics Modelbuilding
Alexander Schilling
ISBN 978-3-0346-1331-6

Basics Technical Drawing
Bert Bielefeld, Isabella Skiba
ISBN 978-3-0346-1326-2

Available as a compendium:
Basics Architectural Presentation
Bert Bielefeld (ed.)
ISBN 978-3-03821-527-1

Construction

Basics Concrete Construction
Katrin Hanses
ISBN 978-3-0356-0362-0

Basics Facade Apertures
Roland Krippner,
Florian Musso
ISBN 978-3-7643-8466-1

Basics Glass Construction
Andreas Achilles,
Diane Navratil
ISBN 978-3-7643-8851-5

Basics Loadbearing Systems
Alfred Meistermann
ISBN 978-3-7643-8107-3

Basics Masonry Construction
Nils Kummer
ISBN 978-3-7643-7645-1

Basics Roof Construction
Tanja Brotrück
ISBN 978-3-7643-7683-3

Basics Timber Construction
Ludwig Steiger
ISBN 978-3-7643-8102-8

Basics Steel Construction
Katrin Hanses
ISBN 978-3-0356-0370-5

Available as a compendium:
Basics Building Construction
Bert Bielefeld (ed.)
ISBN 978-3-0356-0372-9

Professional Practice
Basics Budgeting
Bert Bielefeld,
Roland Schneider
ISBN 978-3-03821-532-5

Basics Project Planning
Hartmut Klein
ISBN 978-3-7643-8469-2

Basics Site Management
Lars-Phillip Rusch
ISBN 978-3-0356-1607-1

Basics Tendering
Tim Brandt, Sebastian Franssen
ISBN 978-3-7643-8110-3

Basics Construction Scheduling
Bert Bielefeld
ISBN 978-3-7643-8873-7

Available as a compendium:
Basics Project Management
Architecture
Bert Bielefeld (ed.)
ISBN 978-3-03821-462-5

Urbanism
Basics Urban Analysis
Gerrit Schwalbach
ISBN 978-3-7643-8938-3

Basics Urban Building Blocks
Thorsten Bürklin, Michael Peterek
ISBN 978-3-7643-8460-9

Building Services/
Building Physics
Basics Lighting Design
Roman Skowranek
ISBN 978-3-0356-0930-1

Basics Room Conditioning
Oliver Klein, Jörg Schlenger
ISBN 978-3-7643-8664-1

Basics Water Cycles
Doris Haas-Arndt
ISBN 978-3-7643-8854-6

Basics Electro-Planning
Peter Wotschke
ISBN 978-3-0356-0932-5

Available as a compendium:
Basics Building Technology
Bert Bielefeld (ed.)
ISBN 978-3-0356-0928-8

Landscape Architecture
Basics Designing with Plants
Regine Ellen Wöhrle, Hans-Jörg Wöhrle
ISBN 978-3-7643-8659-7

Basics Designing with Water
Axel Lohrer, Cornelia Bott
ISBN 978-3-7643-8662-7

Available at your bookshop or at
www.birkhauser.com

Series editor: Bert Bielefeld
Concept: Bert Bielefeld,
Annette Gref
Translation from German into
English: Hartwin Busch
English copy editing: Susan James
Project management: Silke Martini
Layout, cover design, and
typography: Andreas Hidber
Typesetting: Sven Schrape
Production: Amelie Solbrig

Paper: PlanoPlus, 120 g/m^2
Printing: Hubert & Co GmbH & Co. KG

Library of Congress Control Number:
2018939211

Bibliographic information published by the
German National Library
The German National Library lists this publica-
tion in the Deutsche Nationalbibliografie;
detailed bibliographic data are available on the
Internet at http://dnb.dnb.de.

ISBN 978-3-0356-1602-6
e-ISBN (PDF) 978-3-0356-1581-4
e-ISBN (EPUB) 978-3-0356-1604-0
German Print-ISBN 978-3-0356-1562-3

© 2018 Birkhäuser Verlag GmbH, Basel
P.O. Box 44, 4009 Basel, Switzerland
Part of Walter de Gruyter GmbH, Berlin/Boston

9 8 7 6 5 4 3 2 1
www.birkhauser.com